hear me

As I Whisper

to you

KT Brook

BookReality
Helping Writers Become Independent Authors

Published: 2022 byThe Book Reality Experience

Leschenault, Western Australia

ISBN: 978-1-922670-88-5 - Paperback Edition

ISBN: 978-1-922670-87-8 - E-Book Edition

Cover Design by Brittany Wilson | Brittwilsonart.com

"This book is dedicated to those who have been closest to me throughout all the love, companionship, trials and heartache as we embrace the negative aspects of ourselves and others as our tools to learn, grow and embrace all that we are.

To my lifelong partner Steve,

for all he has given me in all that I have become..."

Table of Contents

Hear Me

As I Whisper To You

Through the Eternity

Of The Ages...

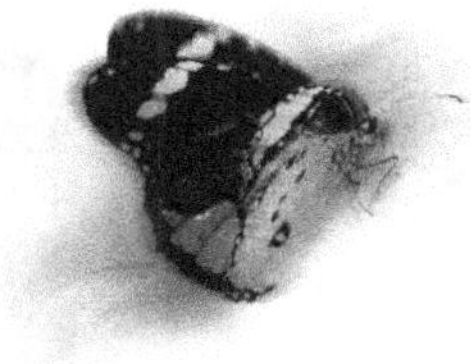

Remembering

Let me speak to you of moments of infinity
from another land.
Feel me - as I wipe the dust of breath across your lips
from a grain of sand,
Stop, as I wipe the memories of your soul to your brow.
Hear me as I linger like a lost memory –
treasured and forgotten,
Caress me as an unknown love.

Remember me, as I remember you
deep within the swell of a thousand years.
Release me through the invisible gates of your past
Shine in the openness of eternity
with your arms open wide,

Love me – as I love you.

Let the waters of a thousand oceans lap
at the gateway to your soul.
Let me dance with gossamer wings
of love across your heart.
Let your softest breath open
the deepest recesses of your mind.
Let the light of the smallest star
guide your path.

Hear me as I hear you...

A gentle dove dost fly

whilst mountains nestled in a sea of blue

spill a gentle breeze through rivulets of deep ravines,

brushing gently, whispering

through the leaves of a field of memory.

Lift me up on high,

embrace a love not yet lost,

glean the sun of warmth on skin.

My mind does not sleep,
it stands on tiptoe on the edge of darkness,
billowing in the flutter of an eyelash.
Let go and one plunge into the dark.

To fall or fly?
But which to choose?
The choice is mine
and the answer lies within.

Seek - but how?
I feel the search inside my heart and soul.
Find the answer and you will find God -
I Am.

Come unto me as I see you kneel

across fresh pastures of your mind.

Hold within your heart the longing of another kind.

Stand in the freshness of the earth beneath your soul.

Awaken to your knowledge of your past.

Kiss the present with your lips,

softly caress what comes with the presence of your breath

Open your heart to the fullness of your knowing.

Discover your love...

Embrace.

Remember the love of a thousand kinds
is softer than a raindrop on a petal.
Do not limit your love
but spread it far and wide.
Let it rest gently upon those that expect it least
and caress the moments it lingers on.
Keep your love close to you in thought and action.
Let it touch your soul and in turn
your soul will touch you.

Brush your love carelessly against a stranger.
Kiss your love with its breath.
Give your love humbly on bended knee.
Offer it in the palms of your hands.
Throw your arms open to love
and drench yourself in its beauty.

Sing love's praises and walk joyously in its glow.

Hear love drench the earth

in the downpour of a summer rain

and sparkle in the winds of winter snow.

Love is here and love is now...

Rejoice in its home in your heart and fear not!

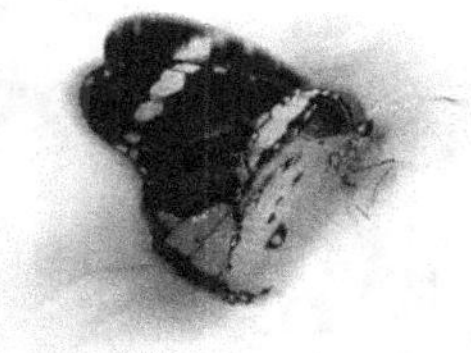

Reconnecting

I walk in the light of love,

I linger in the perfume of the day,

I tiptoe on the edge of night.

I bathe in the feet of humility,

I waft across your sleep,

I am the whisper you thought you saw...

I Am

I walk upon the softly tread path,

I peek through shadows of trees.

My heart beats through the journey

of a thousand stars.

I hold you within and love you without.

I cup your tears in the palm of my hand,

I catch your laugh in the breath of my soul,

I hold you nestled in the lap of time.

Look toward that which you know.

Don't discard the thought of memory.

Hold your hand out to receive

and I will hold mine out to give.

Walk upon the softly tread path,

peak through the shadows of the trees.

You will find me.

Let me hold your hand
as we sit and wander through the memories of our lives.
Let us not linger on the painful memories of the past,
but caress them with our love.

Let our eyes light up with the moments of
laughter and joy that dance across our minds.

Let us remember together and
remind each other.
Let me hold your hand.

Remember when
we became friends and it was infinite and limitless.
Remember when
friendship wasn't dampened by a summer rain.
Remember when
our laughter echoed through the days and nights.
Remember when
We swore our adventures would never end
and the memories would live on forever.
Remember when
the laughter died and the memories faded.
Remember when
you wondered about that friendship of so long ago.

Remember with no remorse.
Remember with fond thoughts and gratitude.
Remember with a smile that dances
at the corners of your mind.
Remember the adventures and the laughter.

Remember fondly of a moment in time

bound tightly in your heart.

Remember when...

I stand in corners or drift past you in a mist,
I hear you when you think of me.
I remind you of something you do not know,
Yet I touch you gratefully.

You know you must and think you can,
reach out to me and find the man
who'll hear your cry and comfort your mind.
I hear you when you think of me.

Lost beneath the ocean wave lies the body of a soul.
Alone and unknowing, recumbent upon the sand
lies the soulless being.

Where did they become lost?
How did they lose the touch of each other?

Life is fraught with the danger of distance...
A whisper, a shout, a journey, a song.

A life lost in thought...
A moment captured in a memory.

Quiet the mind and honour the quest.
Heed the message.
Grasp the chord that binds.

Know each other.

As you walk the softly tread path

Look not toward that which strays your eyes and mind.

Hear the whisper of a thousand trees.

Listen to the hearts of a thousand minds.

Chase not the pace of speed

but instead linger on the depths of hearts reaching.

Who Am I?

I am a being of all possibilities.

There is no right and there is no wrong.

I am an infinite being of infinity.

I am a memory,

I am knowledge,

I am a breath,

I am love,

I Am.

The acid tongue bites drawing temporary acquiescence from those
less prone to fight.
The dragon commands it's courtiers
with forceful arrogance.

But soon the chatter of voices become distant and dim.
The fire in her eyes mist over with the dullness of the days that bleed
into one.
Where have they all gone she muses
as she lifts her arm to command.
She hears them whisper
"We love you but have to go...
See you soon."

"But wait," she pleads, then shouts "Oh Go!"
She surveys her dusty castle, empty and lifeless.
They love me...
They will come back...

I watch and wait,

sitting cross-legged in a chair.

I hear your thoughts & feel your dreams,

sitting cross-legged in a chair.

I shift into your body and your mind.

I watch and wait.

I am your witness, I am your soul.

I watch and I wait,

sitting cross-legged in a chair.

Seek deep into the truth of your heart,

know that which fills your body of a thought, a memory.

Grasp your knowing.

Hold onto what you remember.

Let not the days of life bleed away your memory.

Hold each moment in your hands, your heart, your mind.

Hold it gently, like a firefly that brings

life to that which you know.

Let that which does not serve release

with a warm breath of love.

Find your heart - Your memory - Your soul.

The hardest path of action is inaction.

I lay at your feet that which you do,

reflection of a moment held in the sands of your life.

Observe - Learn - Release.

I Am, you are - a witness.

Hear the beauty and recognise your fear.

Forgive softly and heal fiercely.

As I remember -I feel your sorrow...

As I remember - I feel your pain...

As I remember - I feel your joy...

As I remember - I feel your love.

As I remember - I hear your laughter...

As I remember - I hear your soft words...

As I remember - I hear your name...

As I remember...

I tiptoe on the edge of darkness,

I scream into the night,

I bathe my tears in the pit of black.

I bundle my fears in the unfurling petals of a red rose,

I lay my truth at your feet,

I rest gently on a ribbon of white light.

My breath wafts through the mists of a summer rain.

You know me.

I blew the mist of a thousand butterflies
that kissed the earth on gossamer wings
of beauty and love.

Spread far and wide
the message of journeys yet passed.

I whisper stories through dusty pages of parchment

for you to find.

I call your mind back to another time.

Listen and you will hear the memories

so far and yet so near.

I call you now to hear your story -

To bring your mind forward.

Go forth and lead.

You can't do anything if you don't speak.

Who are you to lie down?

Hand it up and hear God's word.

I have it here.

The answer lies within.

Release the mind and hear the heart.

The path is theirs

The cross is yours.

Heed not the calling of the words.

Look not without but look within.

Hear my call.

Pity those that cannot rest

Triumph serves an empty plate.

I am ever more committed to living honourably

in the light of love.

To serve my highest good and to

recognise my teachers in all their forms and wisdom.

My eyes and heart will lead and

ego will be the knock on the door of

awareness and learning.

Farewell and hello to a wonderful person,

a gift to us all.

If I sit here underneath the olive tree
will you speak to me?
Will I hear the memories and learn
the lessons of my past?
Will you comfort me?
Will you help me to mend my bridges
and shine my light for me to see?

As I ponder the memories and dark recesses,
will you guide me to fill the darkness and make me whole?

If I sit for just a moment...
If I hear you speak...
You will comfort me...

Recovery

The chrysalis of joy wept at her feet,
not tears of sadness but raindrops of happiness
that trickled rivulets of gold bathed in the
light of the bluest sky and warmth of the day.

Water softly caressed her thoughts
and washed away all she didn't need -
as she lay on the body of her soul.

I feel the togetherness & unity

of myself as one with the I Am.

I need not speak and need not fear,

I stand as one in the comfort of love

I live in the moment of now,

I exist without want.

In the dark of the night
When the trees whisper softly on the wind
and the stars light the sky with their powdery sparkle,
I see you deep within my soul
and I hear you murmur.

I wrench my thoughts and steel my resolve
to know what it is that I must face -
what it is that I do not want to see...

Help me to caress the memory - to heal the pain.
To bring forth the light of tomorrow from eternal night
and piece together memories of the past
which then breathe light to new beginnings.

The journey back to who I am

is fraught with the thought of retrospect.

It is too easy to look without and not within.

For the path may be long and painful.

But...

It is for me to grasp the courage of self.

It is only for me to gently hold

and caress myself.

It is to know who

I AM.

When travelling through life's remembrances,

Small stops are but dalliances along the way.

Like dancing in the summer sun

And sheltering from the winter rain.

We laugh, we love, we cry,

Our hands slowly slip from loving embrace

As we whisper our goodbye...

So many words and thoughts
swell and catch in my throat.
I scramble as I try to reach
so many memories in but a moment.
Which one to grasp?
Why do we try to hold on so tight?

Let me let you go
with love, blessing and light.
Memories are presents
that linger long after you are gone -

These are the things that I will hold.

I lay *Peace* at your *feet*,

I bathe your soul in the waters of *Forgiveness*,

I wrap you in the embrace of *Understanding*,

And I hold you in the arms of *Love*.

Let me wipe *from* your brow the memories of *Sadness*,

Let me hold your hands *from* the pain of *Hurt*,

Let me lead you to the gates of *Release*,

And let me lead you to *Me*.

The Mirror

She knelt on bended knee and
declared her undying love.
With open arms and fearless words,
she said "I Love You".

Her eyes softened and her mouth smiled,
peace settled within her every being
and she was home.

She knew her love had been waiting
but never strayed or waivered.
The one person who knew her down
to the depths of her soul.
Who held her in the embrace of
unconditional love and knowing.
No matter what her perceived failures were
her love was complete.

A warm comfort spread throughout

as she turned from the mirror to begin anew.

It seems to be and seems to me
that everything works in synchronicity.
It is only a moment and only a thought
of acceptance and trust
that all is as it ought.

To hand it up and let it go...
Control is an illusion,
unabated ego a delusion.

Throw judgement out the window.
Instead,
grow in humility of self
and wonderment of love.
Trust that everything is as it should be -
beholden unto me.

I slip into your body and fit you like a glove,
you feel my presence and you feel my love.
I am your body, your mind, your soul.
Release yourself to me and I will make you whole.

Look not toward the dalliances of the past,
nor the uncertainty of the future.
Feel the infinite moment of the sun on your skin
and the wind in your hair.
There is nothing to resolve and nothing to fear.

You exist in all moments.
You love through all existence.
You are all of me and I you.

Let us not gleefully laugh at others
as they wander through the desert of confusion
brought on by control and anger.

Instead, let us humbly share their
load and drink from the same cup
of compassion and love.

For we are all one as are they.
What hurts us hurts them.

Search for the olive branch of
peace and calm.
and let this be your guide.

Ego, expectation and duty
hold no ground here.
Let God's light be your beacon
and your strength.

As I wander through the pages of your life

I feel you reaching

to touch a memory in my mind

or caress a window in my heart.

I am gifted with the presence of God every day.

If I speak to him - God will hear me.

I am not alone - I walk in God's footsteps.

Love thyself - and you will love me.

I blast your anger at your body,

I hurl abuse at your throat,

I melt your fists in the fire of revenge.

And yet...

I rise on the wings of freedom,

I bask in the rising of a new day,

I crumble the walls of protection,

And I open my heart to love.

The path is fearsome;

make courage your ally

and joy your companion.

I choose the chrysalis of change -

I am the butterfly of transformation.

I love and I am loved.

YES?

I hear you and know that I am with you.

What is it that you want from me?

Desire. Choose. BE.

Words are just words - BE.

Enlightenment? - BE.

Spiritual? Connected? - BE.

BE with ME - BE Me - and I You.

Release all thought of what may - BE.

Release all expectation - BE.

Just, BE Me.

Walk in Me, Love in Me,

BE - ME.

Memories are not possessions.

Memories serve us.

They serve us to know.

To know is to remember.

Show Yourself!

I show you me every day!

Do not cower behind self-pity.

Stand Up - be fearless!

I rise out of the abyss,
dirty and dusty but triumphant.
The war lasted many years,
with small skirmishes here and there.

Some battles lost and some won.
Were they important?
Who knows now?
The years have wearied the memory.

Wounds were healed
and scars were made.
A tenuous truce the result.

Open hearts strengthen the bond.
Hate, fear and anger left behind.
The sun rises as the day begins anew...

I wish to meet you on the other side
where forgiveness and understanding
rest on thrones of love and light,
and the walls of ego and fear
crumble under the weight of pure love.

I wish to dance with you on the other side
where laughter and joy sparkle in
the light shining on our skin
and we meet in the embrace of remembrance.

I wish to rest in your arms on the other side
where all are one and shine
in the sparkling sun of open hearts.

I wish to open my heart before the other side
so I can feel the joy of love,
that strange and captivating pureness of creation
and recognition that we are not, and never have been - separate.

Your Will Not Mine...

I hand my fears to you,

I rest in your arms (as I have done for many years).

I ask that you sit in my thoughts first and foremost,

for in your guidance and love is true freedom.

Freedom which takes many forms -

freedom from ego, control, insecurity,

hatred, anger and of course - fear.

Freedom which gives love, kindness,

humility, joy, compassion,

patience and laughter.

Your Will, Not Mine.

I hear you whisper to me O' Lord,

I feel your presence,

I wonder at your will,

Free me from my prison of control.

Help me to heed your words

and to follow your lead.

Your will, not mine.

For thine is the kingdom,

the power and the glory,

forever and ever

Amen

I open myself and my heart to God.

I remove all and any blocks to my healing.

I remove all and any blocks to my full empowerment.

I remove all and any blocks to my joy and love.

God has shown me my wounds and removed the sting.

I am healed.

I am empowered.

I am joy and love.

And so it is.

When I sit upon a lonely chair
and speak to people who are not there,
It's me I try to find -
and not the monsters residing in my mind.

I brush them aside,
let them run and hide.
and cup in my hands the warmth of my smile.
Deposit in my soul the light of God,
receive the blessing of the Angels
and live in the honesty of my love.

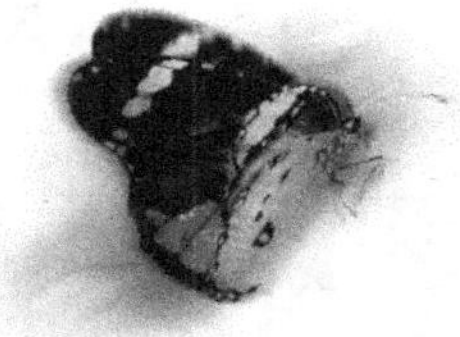

Realisation

Self-Discovery

Discovery of every cell of your being - EVERY cell.

For deep within the memories

is the catalyst for all thought.

Our journey, our discovery of self

is for us to traverse EVERY cell.

To stop and pay attention,

to learn, to discover, to acknowledge,

to release and thank that which no longer serves us.

To document - To KNOW.

Our ascension is a series of steps.

Ascension will only occur through the dedication of self.

I cannot emphasize this enough.

This is important - you are important.

The journey is not easy and you may waiver

but the reward is humbling.

We sit with you, we journey with you.

You are in safe hands.

We start as we mean to finish.
Firmness of words, determination.
There is no room for procrastination!
Do not let the distractions of the outside
hinder the healing of the inside.

You know what you must seek.
Speak it now with strength and courage.
Unresolved wounds fester in the scars
beneath your skin.
Face them, speak your truth so that
your mind can heal...

Am I not ready to forgive?

Is it me that I am not ready to forgive?

I put myself in that position,

I didn't love myself enough to leave.

I thought this treatment was what I deserved.

I thought the abuse was my punishment

for being such a bad, unloved, unwanted person.

I feel like screaming!!!

Dig deeper - there's more.

The journeymen accompany me on the ride,
sitting quietly - there's nothing to hide.
Patiently waiting in the darkness of the shadows,
an outstretched hand a glimmer of light.

A tenuous grasp a small step forward,
the glimmer of hope an acknowledgement of faith,
The path is hidden and the way is shrouded
But step you must and all is forgiven.

From a distant shore I walk your path,

I breathe your life and honour your plan.

The moment is close and the time is now.

I reach out to hold you near,

you feel my presence and heed your purpose.

Understanding is close -

your work begins.

With one hand you receive

and with the other you give (gift).

I touch them through you.

With each gift your heart will heal.

You felt my love once

and will do so again.

I am with you always.

I am in all that I am

I wash my soul in the waters of redemption,
I see beyond my eyes.
I hold all of my heart in the arms of forgiveness,
and I bathe in the world beyond all that I know.

Rest in the moment of understanding.
Languish in the path of least resistance.
Give yourself over to me,
the journeymen await.

She sits upon a lonely stair,
you think, perhaps, some comfort she seeks.
But no, it's only reflection
of memories she contemplates.
A choice, to stand and leave behind
the person she thought she was
and greet her dawn with everything she knows she is.

A breath, a sigh,
she hands herself to trust and love.

I am yours and always have been.
Show me the way and I will follow.

I hear your words, I see you speak,
your comfort rests its arms on my shoulders.
Your presence gives me courage,
and your love fills me with faith.

I listen to and feel my heart -
for this is where you have always been.

The years have been many.
Together we have stayed the course
and emerged triumphant.
Our light is shining and grown ever more.
The work has just begun...

If I could touch someone for just a moment
with the Love of God - I have done my job.

I am Your Hand, Your Voice, Your Messenger.
Through You I reach inside
and hold their heart -
for just a moment...

Of Messengers there are many,

of Voices there are few.

Lean my way,

near me whisper in your ear.

I carry you through

the desert, the rain, the sorrow.

I hear your heart, I hold your soul.

Hand me your heart

and I will hand you love.

Acknowledgements

In gratitude to my table of friends - Anne, Georgie, Michelle and Vanessa for their support and encouragement.

Jackie and Jim Lindsay and my children Joshua and Paige.

Also to those we do not always see but have always known: God, Aunty Lee, Tom, Akira, the Angels, our Guides, and Helen.

About the Author

I am an ordinary person living an ordinary life who has been gifted with words that whisper.

I have a loving partner, family and friends.

At the age of 53 illness forced me to slow down and stop.

To simply breathe was the struggle and has continued to be to this date.

Self-reflection, meditation, breath-work, weekly table sessions with my circle of friends, searching for all the tools and then I began to write...

I journaled, asked myself questions until one day in October 2016, I wrote the words – "Hear Me As I Whisper To You Through the Eternity of the Ages".

It was from this moment that the words began to flow – reaching from forever.

It is my hope that my poetry does not just speak to me but to us all.

In gratitude.

KT Brook, Australia 2022

www.ingramcontent.com/pod-product-compliance
Lightning Source LLC
Chambersburg PA
CBHW072105110526
44590CB00018B/3324
9781922670885